LAST CHILD TO COME INSIDE

Michelle.

Last Child to Come Inside

Michelle Desbarats

HARBINGER POETRY SERIES
an imprint of
CARLETON UNIVERSITY PRESS

Printed and bound in Canada

Canadian Cataloguing in Publication Data

Desbarats, Michelle, date-
Last child to come inside

(Harbinger poetry series ; 6)
ISBN 0-88629-347-2

I. Title. II. Series.

PS8557.E7327L38 1998 C811'.54 C98-901289-1
PR9199.3.D48L38 1998

Cover design and interior: BCumming Design

"Choosing a Counter" appeared in *Graffito* (University of Ottawa) in March 1996, and in *Speak: Six Poets,* from Broken Jaw Press (Fredericton, NB) in 1997. "Intelligent Men" and "Promises" were published in the *Carleton Arts Review* in the Winter of 1997. "Dreaming of You," "In Bermuda," "Morning Glories" and "Lip Marks" were published in *Missing Jacket,* from Above Ground Press (Ottawa), in the Spring of 1997. "Fair," and "Park" appear in *Meltwater,* the forthcoming Banff Writer's Program Anthology (for Fall 1998), from the Banff Centre, AB.

Carleton University Press gratefully acknowledges the support extended to its publishing program by the Canada Council and the financial assistance of the Ontario Arts Council. The Press would also like to thank the Department of Canadian Heritage, Government of Ontario through the Ministry of Culture, Tourism and Recreation, for their assistance.

Harbinger Poetry Series, Number 6

This book is for

Cymbria and Arthur

ACKNOWLEDGEMENTS

I thank my family for their support and creativity, Dave for all we share, Don McKay for his sensitive words and editing, Stephanie Bolster for her gift of rechecking the manuscript many times, Jennie Strickland for her belief in miracles, Richard Taylor who insisted I prepare the manuscript, Christopher Levenson for his support of my work, Olive Senior for the importance of being courageous, Michael Dennis for his encouragement, Bill Kinsella for being my first writing teacher, my friends and fellow-writers for listening, John Stewart for being himself, my father, Peter Desbarats, for memories and my mother, Maggie Desbarats, for her magic.

I also thank the Ontario Arts Council Works in Progress and Writers' Reserve Grant Programs and the Banff Writer's Studio Program for their valuable assistance.

CONTENTS

SMOKING THE GIRL GUIDE BASKET

MY MOTHER'S DESK

GARDEN

GOD AND BRUSSELS SPROUTS

My father loved brussels sprouts,
ordered them for supper.
My sisters and I hated those
vile little green bodies that smelled fiercely
when a fork was jabbed into their softened insides.
They are, now, an innocuous vegetable,
healthy in that dark green way
apparently able to prevent a list of mortalities.
But then, they were abominations beside
the narrow pale bodies of rice
and the meat of the night.
Every Sunday they graced our supper
as God had blessed our bowed heads
at morning church with our father; in time
God and brussels sprouts becoming inseparable.
I'd watch, with eyes of a hawk, and when
my father wasn't looking, I'd let the warm balls
drop from my fingers, to roll under the table.
Even the cat, nosing one, would walk away,
confirming my suspicion of evil.
Years later, my sisters and I discovered
we'd all done this, that every Sunday evening,
on the carpet beneath the table,
floated a sea of small round greenness.
And later, I found out that my mother
had crouched there, on her hands and knees,
gathering the brussels sprouts,
closing out Sunday with this final benediction.

GARDEN

As a child I didn't know
that Playboy magazines on our coffee table
for me to look at
wasn't a situation found in every home.
Mine had books by the great writers
and art books of lands and bodies
and Playboy magazines which I cuddled up with
in the corner of our green and blue floral couch.
Wide eyed, I turned the shiny pages
of delicious women,
round balls of flesh rising from their chests,
hair where I had none,
the look in their eyes of doing something,
even I could tell, they were going to get
spanked for later.
My parents passing around me,
distant benevolent entities.
It was a garden, populated by four eared Eves
with bunny tails, the world I was going
to grow up in,
where, anytime I wanted, I opened the fridge,
lifted out, with my hands the color of seashells,
the beautiful hard body of an apple.

THE TRAPEZE

Sun running across green metal
miracles for climbing,
swings to take one up for a glimpse
of what, to an untrained eye, looked like Heaven
and smelled like it too.
My dad would push me so high
I thought I'd go over the bar
and come straight crashing down.
Not so high, I'd yell and he'd laugh and push.
Once he lifted me up on the little trapeze then
he said let go of your hands and hang
by your knees, I've got you and I did
and he let go, walked away while I yelled
from my upside down mouth, get me down.

EVERY NIGHT SLEEPING WITH THE NAILED DOOR

There was a second door in my bedroom
that my father nailed shut,
sealing its edges to the frame, saying,
we can't have her running wild
about the house in the night.

In the dark, my cheek against painted wood
as I tried to pull out the nails, their rimmed heads
sharp beneath my fingers,
warm salty wetness running into my mouth,
edges of the door, red with wanting.

THE BIRTHS OF MY SISTERS

The small soft bodies of my sisters
dropped from her body as she walked,
as she breathed.
I like to think my birth was different,
accompanied by splendor
and music,
not an everyday event.
I grew afraid to look at her
and all those falling bodies.
Once I saw her stare at the tissue
she'd just used to wipe herself
as though searching for an
impossible thing.
I asked her what it was.
She said nothing.
Now I know she was looking for
the blood of her freedom,
trying to create with her eyes
what her body would not.
Which of my sisters, that day,
hung upside down
like a tiny pink bat, wings folded,
eyes closed, from her interior ceiling.

DOING MAKEUP

My friend learned to put on makeup
from watching her father, a funeral director,
apply it to the faces of dead women.
She'd sit for hours at his elbow
studying as he smoothed blush over
their white cheeks, chose eye shadow that
would have made them, in life, sparkle,
turn heads, make people dream of them
at night. She said her dad was the best.
I remember his long narrow fingers, could
picture him pulling a shade of lipstick
across a silent mouth, moist now
as spring.
Her own face was pale as
a white moth's wing,
she'd sketch out shades for hours
on small pieces of paper before applying them
to her skin,
knowing before she went out
she'd have to pass like the others
beneath her father's gaze.

CHERRY BELLY

They chase her
to the ground,
her thin arms waving
among the whites of their eyes, flash
of green sweater,
her calls reach the edge of the field
run up tree trunks into the branches.
Long brown grass falling beneath their bodies
as they pull up her shirt
cherry belly cherry belly
hammering on the flat of her stomach
their hands raining down again and again.
Finally they get up, leaving her,
grass tops parting before their long strides.
Later I touch the place where she'd lain,
between criss cross blades and flattened wheat stalks
the earth is dark brown, cool moist
to my fingers
as it must have been against her back
while the skin of her stomach burned.

DRIVING

We were sixteen, driving at night
in her dad's car, her slender hands,
pearl polished fingernails, guiding the
steering wheel. We weren't going
anywhere, just cruising past the Y
and run-down houses beside it.
She said, turning her dash lit face toward
mine, that she liked driving with me
because I sat on my own side
not like some of the other
girls who tried to sit
right next to her so their shirts
touched hers, their bare arms rubbed
along her freckled ones, their
cheeks were so close to hers when
they spoke, she could smell
their innocent perfumes, could
see clearly the wet shadow
they'd smudged their eyelids with.
I looked at the shadowed vinyl
section of seat between us,
while the car purred slowly along
night streets. Until then, I hadn't thought
about loving her, whose pale skin
seemed to be made
of a different substance than mine.

BOX RIDE

One of the things we used to love to do
after mom went grocery shopping
was take the large cardboard box
the food had been delivered in;
we'd haul it up to the top of our stairs,
my sisters and I, we'd make sure there were
no staples or nails sticking up inside.
Then we'd all get in, or as many of us
as could fit and wait for a moment at the top,
our heads poking up, our fingers clutching the rim.

Then rock to the edge, closer, closer,
until the front tipped forward,
no stopping now as we shot down
barely touching the front edge of each stair
yelling, the corner, the corner,
hands out then pushing away oncoming wall
box sides leaning, caving,
we've made the corner
now the long stretch, can barely see the end,
banister bars a blur of white.

Will we make it or
pitch headfirst before the finish —
here it comes, the bottom of the stairs,
we fall in a heap but we've made it
the box just holding together till the end.
Mom comes in, drawn by the noise,
or perhaps the sudden silence,
hands on hips, I told you not to do that
you could have been killed,
what if, what if.

But next week we wait
for the grocery truck, run quick as lightning,
box in tow, as soon as it's emptied, to our mountain.
The late afternoon sun is throwing panes of light
onto the faded flowered carpet;
barely discernible dust diamonds ride these shafts.
The air has just a hint of crispness.
The cardboard box is solid and smells of
speed that has only been dreamt of —
it's a fine day for seeing if we'll live to eat supper.

COUNTRYSIDE SO GREEN

In the countryside so green,
with flowers in the gardens
placed like laughter,
there are these beautiful little archways
and miniature houses
so carefully built.
Where did they find those sticks,
so delicate and white and smooth,
as though collected
from trees grown in heaven?
When you go closer you see
that the little branches are bones,
the smaller ones no larger
than a child's.

LOBSTER SUPPER PARTY

Before supper, my father drawing a chalk circle
on the floor and placing the live lobsters in it; the betting
beginning, the cheering for which one would reach
the perimeter first, the lobsters clacking their
hard shells across wood, trying to get back to
the ocean from downtown Montreal,
believing they could
beneath the cries of encouragement.
Then quickly cooked so nothing was lost,
not this last thought inside their tiny brains
to return home, message running into the meat
even into the sweet strings inside shelled legs;
this is what was eaten.
Afterwards there'd be dancing, wild dancing,
I'd watch from behind the banister bars
bodies dissolving into tongues of flame
knowing it was the Holy Spirit drawn to my
parents' dining room
by the faith of lobsters,
their cracked red claws piled on platters on the table
hard shells emptied of soft white prayers.

THE PARK

Don't ever tell your mother this, said my aunt
but once when I took your little sister to the park
I turned my back, just for a moment
and she was gone,
where she'd been was sidewalk, grass, trees.
There were three directions I could go
to find her, I knew I only had one chance,
one choice, I took a deep breath and walked
toward the corner. I didn't run
because I knew if she was around it she would be there
and if she was not, it wouldn't make any difference.
And there she was, in her yellow sunsuit
walking, as proud as could be, along the sidewalk.
I was so happy, said my aunt, I think I cried.

As I listen to her tell me this I read in her face
what the years in-between
have not removed.
A part of my aunt died that day as surely
as the other two little girls, yellow dressed,
that went walking down those other paths
and were never seen again.

LIP MARKS

CHRISTMAS ORNAMENT

My sister ate a red glass
Christmas ornament
then hid behind
the washing machine.

I found her crouched,
tiny blood-coloured slivers
ringing her lips
with glittering sharpness.

In the whites of her eyes
the determination
to stay hidden
until she'd been forgotten.

Crying, she would only say
it became impossible
to keep its beauty
from her mouth.

LIP MARKS

Mouth on a pane
of glass frosted with ice
making lip marks that I can
see a wavy world through.

Sticking my tongue
into the creases of tree bark,
jumping when a wet point
meets mine.

Turning around, reaching
turning again
touching the same thing
from a different direction.

Letting a kitten suck
the small point of my nipple,
its tiny milk teeth
sharp as whispers.

SLICED PEACHES

Sliced peaches
against my lips,
orange brilliant wetness —
if I could tell it to you,
wrap their liquid in words
so thin that
the gold shows through and
juice drips out
onto your fingers ...
afterwards, licking them,
you would taste the sweetness.
Would you read words
that left your fingers wet
with their liquid
then yours?

DESIRE

I am a child
in the ways of it
for it's all I want to do
not with everyone but you
who touch me.
You touch me, it's then I
know I want you to touch
me more, your touch on my
skin opens my wings
all moist from being held close,
your touch makes my teeth shine,
pulls the covers from my chest,
makes my body shiver —
and I want to touch
thin veil of skin that
holds you in the world, touch
underneath this, suck the edges
of your heart,
trace a line to
where it all starts and ends,
where the sun sets,
leaving between your legs
the rising of the first night.

MORNING GLORIES

A profusion of morning glories
in a heavy rain,
if you were here —
close my eyes — I would think of them
and kiss you.
Your lips would be the blue edged
petals, I would move my mouth,
give me wet blue between deep green,
my cheeks slippery with rain,
my eyelashes dark-joined with water.
If you were here I would press my face
to your neck,
smell the darkness of your sweater.
I know it would rise to my nose
like the smell of sidewalks in the rain,
something hot and dry becoming wet,
I've always loved that smell.

VISIT

I touch
the petals of my skin, velvet
of my tongue, small knives
of teeth I can use at will;
my nipples, tiny red coals that slowly burned
two holes in all my shirts.
She searches for me
muttering, that her daughter
is here somewhere,
spark that jumped from
her body, began
making tiny scorched circles
on the rug, on the sofa, wherever
I landed.
My mother used to smoke,
I blamed these marks on her.
Now I know it was me burning up
her furniture. She's calling me
to come out again,
searching for that acrid
tinge of smoke that stings eyes, makes
the heart want to bite and swallow.
My mother walks through her house,
humming the burning song. I see
it starting, whispers of smoke rising
from my fingertips on her dining table.

FIRE

We read the books
in her bedroom,
pink burning the fair skin
beneath her freckles,
my face hot to touch.
Books in plain yellow covers
she'd found
in the basement,
hid them under her bed.
That night she was wakened
by the raging heat
of a fire swallowing her covers.
She escaped through a tunnel of flame
down the stairs,
stood barefoot on pavement
dark with running water
and snaking lines of hoses
while the blaze tore
orange red into the sky.
She told me the fire had started
in the books under her bed.
I said that wasn't true
but later, the first time she made love
her house burned down again.

THE DEAL

That we found each other —
doesn't that speak to you of destiny?
That in all this wide world
my bent soul and yours
fit together to form the particular
structure of death,
our outer skins hiding this.
Though we're hated, they will wonder
how it was for us
when our bodies came together, it will
not leave them quiet; our capacity for
depravity will become legend,
groans that fled our mouths
at what cost.
We were magnificent together,
leading each other further
than either had crept alone.
When we killed I could feel
meat shuddering along my bones —
was it good for you —
that I would do anything for you was
the beginning of your genius.

Without you
my life is cut, half my feelings,
half my taste, half the pleasure
screaming from the white hot pain inside,
gone — not the half of others;
ours was so immense.
That was the deal I made to save my body.
With you was when I lived,
they will remember us together for eternity.
Alone, I am a spectre, and you
lose your beauty among men.

THE NIGHT PICASSO BECAME MY RED VELVET DRESS

The night Picasso became my red velvet dress
he said to draw him onto my body.
I said, with you everything is draw, draw.
Just do it, he said.
So I did, not because I am agreeable or it
was Picasso but because it was a beautiful night.
I slid him over my arms, pressed him against
my stomach, smoothed him at my hips. I said
you think you are getting something from me,
you're not. I brushed my hair, arching
my back as I raised my arms. He said
lift your left arm a little higher, like so,
there, now hold that don't move. I said
I'm not standing still for anyone, not even you.

Y.

You won't allow me to speak
unless my words are trimmed
with lace.

You won't allow my tears
unless they are the sort caught
on fingertips.

Somewhere, but I can't remember —
I grew a sadness bigger than
my body.

SOMEONE IN THE UPSTAIRS APARTMENT

I wake and know it is far too early;
the air against the darkened wall
has the look of being in the same room
with someone who is sleeping.
It does not acknowledge my presence
but remains inert, back turned to me
its head tucked under its wing.

Everything is so quiet, if you
opened your mouth then closed it
you could taste the silence on your tongue,
the barest hint of chalkdust,
color of midnight wax,
and into this, drifting down, an invisible sporadic rain,
the sound of someone crying, upstairs.

THE COLLECTOR

If anyone collected things, he did,
from furniture to the tiniest piece of glass
all arrayed in his home. I used to be afraid
of losing things, he said.
But now, his marriage ending, he's selling
bit by bit to buy a freedom
somewhere in the woods.
I've come to realize, he said, that there
will always be beautiful things,
now I have to let go of them but later
I will have them again, they will find me.
I think of him, years from now,
in a cabin from which no trail winds
and wonder if things of beauty
can indeed, as he says, forge their own paths
to those of us who love them.

DREAMING OF YOU

I thought I would dream of you when
the brightness was quick within me.
But it's now, when the tide has gone out
leaving sandbars aching in nudity
and then the water's come back in
covering them, touching the thin green
bodies of grass at the banks.
When all that has happened,
I dream of a meeting I'm to go to
where you are and at the same time
you're here with me.
I wake to your fingers
speaking to me in the pale bone poetry
of the language for the deaf.

But these could be the wings of birds
and an entirely different situation.

NIGHT FOR FALLING

It's a night for meeting the man of your dreams,
sure it is, the air smells like clover honey;
everywhere you look there is that perfect violet
shadow being cast by something.
It runs up someone's face and you think, there
he is, it's the moment you've been
living toward, you would have
recognized him anywhere because he's wearing
just what you'd planned for him
in your fantasies. Your gaze meets his,
of course, this is the man of your dreams.
The conversation flows like water, you think
it's so easy to talk to this person, in fact you have
the uncanny feeling of knowing just a fraction of
a second ahead of time what he's going to say,
and he does, he says it all. In three minutes
you are sharing more than with people
you've known for years, that doesn't scare you
because you suddenly realize with him
you are depthless, talk will just continue
flowing, you've never known this about yourself,
had poured out your knowledge in measured
increments, it's the same for him, you are
inseparable; from this moment
it feels like heaven has descended.
You look away for a second, see the purple
shadow fall across the cheek of a man not far
from you. He turns his head, your gaze meets his,
of course, he is the man of your dreams,
all your life you have been living for this.
It is that kind of night.

WALKING IN THE DESERT

After supper he says
he thinks he'll go out
walking in the desert
for a while.
When he returns
he has sand in his hair,
grains of fine dust
cling to the prickly shadow
of his cheeks,
a wild look to his eyes
of not seeing water
for days.
The night, he says, is exquisitely
stark, the sky hanging
huge above the dunes;
the ceiling so high
all light is lost
with distance
so that his face
was touched only
by falling dark.
A single strand of hair
winds, like a camel's trail,
across his forehead
where the madness glitters,
a jewel he does not yet
want to let go.

MEN'S COATS

I believe a man's skin is made of dark fabric
that comes below his knees
and that he doesn't have two nipples but many
buttons down the front from his neck
to his lower edge.
I believe the skin he shows me
with a penis between his legs
is just what he wears
because he's shy
but that if I can find out how
to undo this I'll find his real skin
to feel against my body,
its soft coarseness pressing a
patina onto me, each button
another hardness to rub myself on
until I come again,
my hands deep in his deep pockets
keeping them warm
as we both lay down on the ice
that always forms beneath a man's real skin.

TASTE

A man, after having his appendix out,
lost his sense of taste
due to a reaction to the anesthetic, they told him.
He was very unhappy, said his wife,
sometimes he'd come home, she'd be cooking
a roast, and he'd go so crazy with grief
he'd have to run out of the house.
Then after an operation for his heart,
they were sitting, eating spaghetti one night,
when he said quietly to her,
Norma, this tastes good.
She put down her fork, staring at him
as he cut through the noodles,
raising the steaming forkfuls
to his mouth.
She said, my God, you have
your taste back, this is incredible.
For today, he said, I have it for today.
And then, she said, she could see,
in the light of the candle they'd lit for the meal,
that he was crying.

SMOKING THE GIRL GUIDE BASKET

LUNCH

Look out
I'm eating broccoli soup
right out of the pot on the stove,
feeling the heat of the burner
warming my cheeks,
tasting the hot liquid that
lies right next to the bottom.
I'm eating a sandwich
before I ever set it down onto
the plate, I'm just making it
and eating it
and now
I'm eating the red insides out of
the end bowl of watermelon,
no neat little slice here,
I've got juice gathering
in the holes I'm scooping out,
like when you dig
below the waterline.
Just yesterday I was
sucking meat out of lobster legs
squeezing it toward my mouth with my teeth
through the red straw-thin shell.
Give me a bone and I'll
hit something with it before I bite on it
because in the wild, where I am,
nothing tastes so good as when
it's been used first to protect oneself.

PEAS

I like the idea of eating peas
after they've been used to kill someone
because it just goes without saying
it would take a lot of peas
to snuff someone,
finally after a constant
bombardment, they go crazy, die
and I like peas, sitting down
with a whole mound of them, hot
butter making them slippery.
Maybe someone could kill someone
with one pea shot hard and fast to
a crucial area on the neck
or forehead,
one deadly pea,
but I wouldn't be interested in
getting to know that person,
they wouldn't have a sense of the
abundance of things.

WHEN I LIVED AMONG BIRDS

You say there is a way of turning words to sound:
I give you three, watch as you draw
their letters into notes among
lines you've made, listen to you forming
soft sounds — no longer words but a rising and falling
of your voice; realize this is what I first must have heard,
just this calling of sounds and that I lived with
birds then. I remember now,
strange featherless birds that flew
near the ceiling,
made circular nests of sheets on top of beds,
filled bathtubs and sinks, dipped
their heads below water surface for food,
their calls in the air and
my answering calls;
the birds helping me. Then slowly
words coming in, like tiny stones rustling together,
then larger, more solid, the music becoming the invisible
thread; words are beautiful, but when
they came, I began to live among people,
not always understood. This is what I remember
as I watch you turn words back to music.

MY GUARDIAN ANGEL IS TEACHING ME HOW TO PLAY POOL

We go after breakfast,
usually I have to wait until he finishes his orange juice,
then we're off;
his long gown trailing behind me,
all that fabric blowing in the wind
and his wings so close they might be mine
if I stepped back a little and he wasn't terrified,
like me, of serious bodily contact.
When I first did this after breakfast, I couldn't
explain why; something invisible taking my
hand, leading me, the intangible pull
somewhere.
It was only after the second game I heard a
voice, like the edges of clouds, say suggestively
try the six in the corner. Then
not quite like that, spin the white ball, and
looking around I saw no one close enough.
I don't know exactly what he's teaching me, only
that there is another language of reciprocal action —
spoken loudly, sometimes so softly like gentle rain,
sometimes working:
locked thud of the ball pocketing; sometimes not:
unreachable deep heaviness of white ball
weighting the first voice,
unmistakable lightness of a triple shot off
the banked side,
irrevocable tome of the eight ball ending the
conversation, sometimes far too soon.
But I'm just learning to speak with the far
end of a narrow stick,
blue dust powdering my fingertips, like the dust
of the sky. I ask him, are there pool tables in Heaven?
He says, *there is one below every star.*

IN BERMUDA

Jesus and Elvis were seen drinking
tequila at a tiny bar
in Bermuda.
Apparently they went for the sun.
Elvis was pale, even by Heaven's standards
and Jesus hadn't had a vacation, a real
leave it all behind you holiday, for
years now.
One of those types who put it off, pile up
all their sick days,
Jesus had enough time stored to be gone
for a long time.
Finally it was God who said, as he threw
Jesus the old swimming trunks, to go, get on
out of here and to take that Elvis with him.

Jesus and Elvis were seen wading
into the water at a small beach
in Bermuda.
Jesus had on a pair of faded green plaid
loose fitting shorts and Elvis had on sunglasses.
Someone apparently asked Jesus, when the ocean
had reached over the waistband of the green
bathing suit, why wasn't he walking on water?
Jesus said that he was doing things differently now,
that the whole water act had been a mistake,
got people off on to the wrong tangent.
After that they had been waiting, always waiting
for the extra things.
Apparently Elvis had said that he knew what he meant,
that he never should have worn his hair like that.

Elvis said that he should have just got a nice
regular haircut, nothing fancy.
Didn't know any better then, said Elvis.
I know, said Jesus, it was the same for me. I was thinking
water, I can walk on it. Now I'm always wondering
what would have happened if I just swam.
Elvis was heading into the deeper water, wetness
slicking his back. Come on, he yelled, or can't you swim?
Never needed to learn, said Jesus.
Just follow me, called Elvis.
He dove and broke the surface like a dolphin.
Elvis cried, I could have been a dolphin,
oh God, I could have been.
And Jesus, a helping kind of guy,
did his magic for him, suddenly.

SMOKING THE GIRL GUIDE BASKET

Wanting to do the smoking thing
but not old enough to buy the stuff,
my sister and I huddle in our closet,
single light bulb on,
unwind a wooden basket I'd made
at Girl Guide camp
forcing straight the narrow tube of wood
between us, coils still imprinted
along its brittleness.
My sister strikes a match, lights the far end
while I pull and suck on the other in my mouth,
nothing happening,
trying again, pulling
with all my lungs.
My sister calling out —
all along its length tiny lines of smoke
rise from invisible vents, drift into the
semi dark air, growing
larger, thicker.
It's on fire, my sister yells
and it is, the whole snaking form
a vehicle of smoke.
Grabbing it, we race to the bathtub,
throw it in, turn on the water.
Well, says my sister, that didn't work,
what shall we try smoking now?

CHOOSING A COUNTER

Was listening to a man talk on the radio
about how to choose your kitchen counter,
realized it was excellent guidelines
on how to choose a husband.
First, he said, decide on the color you want,
what will go with your decor, compliment your walls.
Get them to cut you off a sample, they'll do it
if you look like you're serious.
Take it home and don't be hasty,
it's your lifetime we're talking about.
Put it in different areas of your kitchen,
against the wall, get right down on the floor with it,
see how it goes with the linoleum or whatever you have.
You don't want to change that
once you've installed your selection
and what seems like a minor irritation now
will only get worse under stress.
Check it out at different times of the day,
under various lighting conditions;
first thing in the morning, if it's bad,
it isn't going to get better in a day or two.
Remember, you are the one who's going
to look at it when you wake up.
It's got to be fine in the night
and make a lot of good sense in the day.
Try placing some of your favorite foods on it.
Finally, when you are absolutely sure
this is what you want in your house for a long time,
go to the store and tell them
what length you need.

INTELLIGENT MEN

Intelligent men have at least one
stuffed animal, of which they are
really fond, but
this leaves a vulnerability for attack
on these helpless things by other men.
I have seen Bugs Bunny's long legs
spread wide on a bed, a man crying
at the depravity of this act, another devastated,
his fox submerged in shaving cream,
a man enraged, his panda hung by the neck
from a doorway, a penguin stuffed
headfirst down a toilet,
other terrible things done to
men's stuffed animals for revenge
or boredom.
But I have seen a man learn how
to wash his fox, brush the fur to newness,
bring Bugs Bunny back from indecency's
thin edges, become a leader in his profession.
I have seen him tenderly hold to his chest
something that couldn't love him back,
the desolate beauty of a man
learning to love without asking questions.

BREAD

Anyone can say they spent the night in a house
with a dead person, anyone can say this,
but can anyone say they crept down
past midnight to stand, eating soft white bread,
outside a dining room door, where just inside
on the dining room table, lay a dead person,
dead as stone, dead white as the bread?
I did this because I was hungry.

PENGUINS

Do you know about penguins? I asked.
Sure, he agreed.
That the one nearest the edge, I continued,
gets pushed in so the leopard seal will eat it
while the others go swimming and fishing?
No, he replied, I liked to think of them,
in those little tuxedoes, as being somehow more like us.

FAIR

When the aliens came to town
they'd set up a fairground with rides,
names like the Galaxy Swing,
the Comet. There was a ride that resembled
a ferris wheel but it had stars
all over it, they lit up in the dark
so it looked like a circular section
of the night sky whirling around.
When the aliens came to town they
set up booths selling food called
space travel burgers and
milky way cotton candy. You could buy
a drink called lightspeed that looked
and tasted like lemonade
only sweeter, faster.
When the aliens came to town they all
had fuzzy hair like Albert Einstein,
like cotton candy, they all wore
muscle t-shirts with low hanging arm holes,
they wore jeans, the legs greasy from wiping
wrenches after tightening bolts.
Everything looked different
even outside the fairgrounds,
stop signs glowed like white-lettered poppies,
grass whispered next to sidewalks in the dark.
Money pressed into the pockets of our pants,
we put on pretty blouses leaving one more button
undone, we shivered as strange heavy
fingers pulled worn lines of leather
or black rubber across our hips,
the only protection for rides bringing
us a little closer to the stars.
Afterwards we'd wonder if the aliens loved us,
we'd search their faces,
laugh, move away from their moist grins.

Sometimes a girl went too far for love,
after the rides disappeared and the night had
lifted back into outer space
a half human, half alien child
would be left, growing in the ground
of her stomach,
a child to be afraid of.

MY MOTHER'S DESK

GORDON

Perhaps if he had two good eyes, not one that
wandered under its sagging lid,
revolving in its own universe.
If he wore pants that weren't in danger
of slipping from his crooked hips,
if his thin shirts didn't show so clearly his narrow chest,
his bleak nipples.
If he didn't walk with a slow crazy shuffle
around behind the tennis courts
to search for the balls hit back there,
some of them hers,
that he brought back to her, a grin turning up one
corner of his lips,
perhaps she could have loved him.

It was clear he loved her,
his love as blatant, as easy to read as his brand of cigarettes
showing through the fabric of his
breast pocket.
It lit his face like the sun lit
the waves in the bay.
It was holy as a Sunday
and we did it homage by calling him
her boyfriend, not seriously, not to harm,
just to explain the purity of it
the way his fingers held the fuzzed tennis ball
before he gave it to her,
stumbling across the damp green grass to wait
beside the court.

When we called him her boyfriend, he'd grin,
a bit of saliva flecking his mouth,
and comb back his graying hair.
She'd get mad at us
but never enough to really stop us.
He was a fragile closed door between our mother
and anyone else who might cause her pain,
he was her crooked knight.
The winter he died, we heard, alone
in a boarding house,
spring no longer greeted my mother,
its peculiar shuffle across the green
bringing all the love it could hold
in its one good eye.

NICKELS

I could pull
a nickel from my children's ears
or knees, from among strands
of hair, from skin. They'd laugh
at the soft tug of metal leaving
their bodies. Never knew where
it would erupt from flesh and
bone, only that my fingers
would be there too, guiding its exit,
making sure no trace of hard gray
remained beneath the surface.
That's magic, I'd tell them, flashing
the shining disc before their eyes.
Small hands reaching into thin air,
do it again, they'd ask, and I would,
for as long as they wanted I'd bring
the coins from their bodies.
They'd say, after a while, that there must
be so much money now, on the floor,
somewhere beside where I knelt
a pile of bright nickels for us to spend.
But it seemed these were the kind that
glowed briefly in the short voyage
from my children's surfaces to
my fingers, then disappeared.
I'd tell them, that's magic.
Sometimes I'd see them rubbing the
skin of their bodies, as though searching
with small fingers for the edges
of all the hidden nickels.

JESSICA

Jessica is a hoot, really, a laugh in spite of
breast and lung cancer, pain-filled in her hospital bed
so at times her lips disappear and she doesn't make a sound.
She talks about her and I going out to the casino
and with her five dollars we can make a thousand.
When I tell her I can't drive she swears, says
what the hell good are you.
I talk to her when my mother gets a phone call,
and wants (or I think she wants) privacy, I go to Jessica's
side of the room, as though she will not mind.
Sometimes she'll warn me not to make any noise,
if her program's on, the small screen inches from her face.

Jessica has red hair
and chemo, when I ask about this she says damn
doctor gave her a drug so she'd keep her hair but
the tumor doubled. May as well go bald, she says,
she'll be dead anyway. She's got one breast left and now
there's a lump there. She tells me after she lost her first breast,
(lost, I think, as though she misplaced it behind
the sofa, her fault), that an old veteran came to visit,
sat beside her, talked the whole time about the war.
Why the hell, she yells, that just two days after
her breast was gone did she want to hear about the war
and he wouldn't shut up. Four years later her cheeks still flame.

Jessica wears pink wedge-heeled slippers
that she gave to her mother-in-law but reclaimed
after her death, still perfectly good.
She said she'd bought herself black ones and laughs,
my mother and I know what she means,
that warm sexy laugh from a woman
flat on her back. They're wheeling her out for a bone scan.

She yells out to the attendant not to let the metal bar
over her head fall and kill her. Oh what the hell, she says, let it fall,
and that I can have her pink slippers.
I tell her I want the black.
Sure, she says, you can have both.

The room, after she leaves, is quiet. My mother says she's
feeling low today. In my heart I understand her tiredness of holding
on to precious things that will go, like light at the end
of the afternoon and Jessica.

TAKING

While you touched my back
my skin memorized the small mountains
of your hands,
where the crevices are,
places my feet can stretch to
find ledges,
indents my smaller fingers
can grip onto lines cut in your flesh by streams
freezing and expanding in midwinter,
the smooth places I can lie back against,
my face turned upward into the shearing wind
and the earth scent of them
and where
birds' voices have caught on them,
even the tiny two-note love song of the chickadee:
before I sleep in my own darkness I call
your hands with my skin and they come
to hold me.
Did I take too much
leaving you
fingerless until just before dawn?

PROMISES

Past midnight
could be any hour
the hospital room darkened
and quiet,
now and then the soft passage
of a nurse's feet
on the floor outside the room.
My mother, shrunken, grey,
so unlike herself,
barely is able to lift her
narrowed fingers
to pull the oxygen mask
off her face, says she's tired
has had enough,
lets it slip to her neck
her face turning to one side
tears running down her cheeks.
When she was beautiful
she once held my child small shoulders
pointed to the backyard
tried to make me promise to take her
out there, shoot her
if she got too old or too sick.
Tonight there is just her and I,
in the distance below this window
headlights of cars create
a slowly reconfiguring constellation
in the dark.
I wonder how long it will take
before her brain becomes starved
of oxygen, we wait, finally I touch her arm
lightly, her eyes open.
Together we lift the mask
back onto her face
knowing it is not yet time
to keep the unmade promises.

CALLING THE LOONS

My son can call the loons;
he is just a little child,
fair skin except in summer
when the sun and wind brush colour into it.
I made this child, grew these limbs,
danced and sang to him, my sinews a cradle
catching him within my lake.
I remember him there, making me smile
while he explored his fingers in the darkness
within my flesh,
his eyes sometimes open, seeing inside of me
as I never have.
It is said the child begins to practise things there:
opening, closing the mouth
moving, listening to sounds without images coming
through veined membrane of a first sky.
My son stands by himself on the shore of the lake,
indigo beginning to stain overhead,
a few bright stars.
His back to me, he raises his head, gazes
into the air around him
and calls to the loons
in their language, waits, calls.
In the distance — an answer.
He calls again, they answer;
in the dusk, a dialogue and then from far away
their sleek forms riding the wavelets.
His calls quickening as he sees them, as he
recognizes their forms,
their calls stronger as they swim to him.
My son calling the loons —
how can he do this?

Was he a loon before he became my
child, did he slip among the water's deepness
like a dream
or is there a memory, somewhere in his body,
of calling out to something
beyond what he could see,
believing that it will always answer.

SHOWERING WITH THE JAPANESE

Later, in the shower room, the women stand
pushing silver buttons for streams to cover their bodies;
first one slips the strap of her bathing suit off her shoulder to reveal
unobstructed nakedness then releases her body
from fabric — then we all, and finally the Japanese women
pull their wet blue one piece suits from their skin
and we are all showering, water shining our breasts,
running down stomachs, drenching pubic hair.

I realize it is the clothes that separate us into dryness, here without
bark, we are flesh in the rain
occasionally looking at each other
as we direct courses of water beneath our arms,
turn our backs, open our legs so that it can
find the narrow stream bed high up between.

The Japanese rubbing their fingers over their skin,
eyes half closed dark crescents,
girl in the corner, foaming suds through her curly
hair, the other girl more muscular, creaming her thighs;
I'm the last to go, standing in the rain for a moment longer
among the humid ghosts of the departed bodies,
my skin taking the last thin rivers,
last child to come inside after the call has been sounded.

RED HORSES

Red horses, oh where did you go, I know
you were here, for it was the maple tree —
when she saw your color, she chose it
for her own, in the fall, when the icy wind
blows, to warm her limbs.

Red horses, I know your small fire-hot hooves
pierced the earth, for here and there
a red flower, bright as passion breaks
the green; I can still hear your call on the wind
that blows through my dreams of you.

Red horses, I think it was just after I was born
or long before, as I lay naked, the green grass
nibbling the withins of my body, I was
half asleep in the sun; your red nose nudged my cheek
while I pressed my stomach into the earth.

Red horses, at sunrise and sunset, I can still see
a memory of your running in the crimsoned clouds
that hold the sun. If I sit quiet and close
my eyes, will that bring you near to me
or will you come if I howl until I bleed?

FALL

That fall, thirteen years ago
my daughter, wearing a bright pink
knitted cap with two little pointy ears,
sat in a brown wrinkled sea;
our small fenced yard
had become awash foot deep in leaves.
There I placed her, just six months old,
sitting in among their whispery bodies.
She'd seen spring's green, summer's yellow,
now this; as far as she knew
the seasons never repeated
but unfolded one upon the other,
worlds of unimaginable differences.
She looked at me, figure at the edge
of this now brown land.
Then with a tiny chubby hand she reached in,
pulled out a leaf, touched it
to her cheek, her nose, then finally
delicately opened her mouth and placed
the papery edge against her tongue.
I remember thinking when had I
last brought a leaf to my mouth,
so long ago I couldn't recall but assumed
the taste would be brown and dry.
I didn't taste a leaf then as my daughter did.
But this year, it seems it is she who now stands
on the edge of my field and somehow
I want to place a dried leaf, gift of the fall,
to my mouth, as she did long ago.
It has nothing to do with words
but of something she was trying to teach me
that I took so long to learn.

MY MOTHER'S DESK

Sunlight lays the back of a bright cat
along the carpet, air silent
around it to encourage its sleeping.
My mother, as usual, is in her chair
by the window, the three weeks
she spent in the hospital
are as far away now as she is close.
From the dining room chair
where I sit, I can reach out my hand
touch her.
She asks me, would I like to have her desk,
beautiful roll-top, for as long
as I can remember her domain,
private world in the midst of raising six
daughters herself. Don't touch it, she would say,
do not go in it. We understood and
allowed her only this darkness enclosed
by its oak drawers and shelves.
My mother might have asked me if I want
her body, her flesh, bones, corners of
her mind, branchings I've walked
so long and hard to be away from, showing
her that I can walk alone, showing her
that I will be the immortal one, getting far
enough from the flesh of my birth to ever die.
Now she is calling me home.

The HARBINGER POETRY SERIES, an imprint of Carleton University Press, is dedicated to the publication of first volumes of poetry by Canadian poets. Initially, Harbinger's mandate is to publish two volumes per year; if funding permits, however, it is to publish no fewer than four volumes per year. As the title of the series implies, our mission is to herald poets in whom we have discovered not just the potential for good verse, but an already clear and confident voice.

ALSO AVAILABLE IN THIS SERIES

Holly Kritsch, *Something I'm Supposed to Remember*
"Holly Kritsch is an immediately attractive poet, gifted with the stern voice of raw confession. Telling of harrowing blasphemies against childhood, telling of violation and irrepressible love, her poetry matters." — *George Elliott Clarke*

Ronna Bloom, *Fear of the Ride*
"Few poets write of grief and love with such a simple elegance and an impressive depth. Ronna Bloom writes clear and hard about what hurts, and gives us hope." — *Susan Musgrave*

Anne Le Dressay, *Sleep is a Country*
"Have you heard rocks keening? Anne Le Dressay helps us recognize the sound. Austere as ancient standing stones, her poems are perfectly shaped, perfectly positioned to reflect the wordless light." — *Mary A. Wright*

Mark Sinnett, *The Landing*
1998 winner of the League of Canadian Poets' Gerald Lampert Award for the best first book of poetry published the previous year. "These poems [are] blessedly unphoney and clearvoiced ... quite often piercingly unexpected, moving, right." — *Don Coles*

FORTHCOMING: Craig Poile's collection, *First Crack*